GARDENS OF THE IMPRESSIONISTS
POSTER BOOK

Pomegranate Calendars & Books, San Francisco

Pomegranate Calendars & Books
Box 808022
Petaluma, California 94975

Text and illustration reproductions © 1990 Pomegranate Calendars & Books

ISBN 0-87654-575-4
Library of Congress Catalog Number 90-60333
Pomegranate Catalog Number A557

For more information on Pomegranate's other publications, including books,
calendars, address books, books of days, print portfolios, posters, notecards and
postcards, please write to Pomegranate, Box 808022, Petaluma, California 94975.

Cover design by Bonnie Smetts
Printed in Korea

CONTENTS

INTRODUCTION

"There is implanted in the soul of man an instinctive love for women, children and flowers, so that in considering this subject of Flower Painting under the full light of day we are getting down to the fundamentals. What normal human being can see a garden full of flowers in bloom or a hillside sprinkled with nature's own decorations, the wild flowers, without an emotion of joyful admiration! What, therefore, can be a better subject for a painter than that afforded by almost any village or country garden, pasture or hillside?"
— Charles C. Curran,
The Outdoor Painting of Flowers, 1909

The twenty-seven reproductions of garden paintings gathered in this book represent the essence of one of the most beloved genres of painting ever created. In effect, they tell the story of the Impressionist movement. Originated in the 1860s with the French artists Monet, Renoir, Pissarro, Sisley and Manet, Impressionism represented a break with the past in subject matter, style and technique. The hasty, unfinished appearance of these canvases with their spots and dabs of bright, high-keyed hues provoked ridicule and outrage when they were first exhibited in 1874. The artists were labeled rebels and degenerates. Yet within twelve years, by the eighth and final group show of Impressionist paintings in Paris in 1886, Impressionism drew praise and acceptance from critics and the public. Its success generated a wave of practitioners throughout Europe and America. It reached its peak of popularity in France in the late 1880s and throughout the rest of Europe and the United States in the late 1890s and the early decades of the twentieth century.

The garden was one of the principal subjects of Impressionist painting. Many of these garden paintings are today so well known and assimilated into our collective taste that we may neglect to consider how revolutionary and innovative they were initially. The industrialization of Europe and America in the mid-nineteenth century produced a growing middle-class with ample leisure time. These people sought out the countryside and nature to get relief from the increasingly crowded, noisy and dirty conditions of the city where they lived. Gardening became a popular hobby for the leisure class, sustained by scores of horticultural books and periodicals and scientific advances in breeding new plants and flowers. The French Impressionists, members of this new leisure class, sought their subjects in contemporary life, in the cafés, boulevards and parks of Paris, and in the sun-filled leafy suburbs outside the city (which were, in easy reach, thanks to the development of the railway). These artists adopted *plein air* painting, rejecting traditional landscape painting methods that required work to be finished in the studio following initial outdoor sketches. Conventional style, characterized by dark, sombre canvases that portrayed idealized, often allegorical subjects or social messages, yielded to the Impressionists' light-infused paintings of their own immediate world.

The garden suited the Impressionists' needs perfectly: it was nature civilized and contained, easily accessible and yet private. It was a "controlled laboratory," as Monet said, in which the artist could perform endless experiments, painting outdoors in all seasons and weather conditions, and recording on canvas the fleeting effects of light and atmosphere of the moment.

Figures included in these "gardenscapes" were usually women and children, at their leisure. Their presence functioned as color accents and heightened the effect of harmony and beauty; they were identified with the innocence and tranquility of the natural world. Their manner appeared graceful, not rugged, and they were dressed in the latest Paris fashions. Where men appeared in these paintings, they did so as city dwellers enjoying a respite in the country. No one toiled in an Impressionist's garden.

It was Claude Monet (1840–1926), of all the Impressionists, who was mainly responsible for transforming the suburban garden into the most influential theme in the art of the era. Beginning in 1872, Monet lived in a succession of houses in small towns outside of Paris: Argenteuil, Vétheuil and, at last, Giverny, where he moved in 1883 and remained for the rest of his life. His gardens furnished him and his friends and colleagues with subject matter for hundreds of paintings (*Gladioli* on page 9 depicts Monet's garden in Argenteuil with his wife, Camille, posed amidst the brilliant display of flowers), but the gardens he designed at Giverny were of seminal importance to Impressionism. Monet considered them to be as much a work of art as his painting.

Scores of young artists from all over Europe and the United States visited Giverny, and it soon grew to the status of an art colony. By 1890, Monet had become a celebrity. An observer at the time noted,

> "The village, apparently, was favored by artists even before he arrived; but Monet, his immediate followers, and the constant stream of American visitors transformed it into an artists' colony. Studio skylights appeared on thatched roofs; there were two outdoor cafes, without which French artistic life would have been at a loss; and across the street from the town's one hotel were the tennis courts.... There was the attraction of the Norman countryside.... Then there was Monsieur Monet himself. The 'maitre', big, bearded, and patriarchal, had the kind of personality that attracts disciples."

Frederick Carl Frieseke (1874–1939) moved permanently to France from America at the age of twenty-four and lived next door to Monet at Giverny from 1906 to 1919. Frieseke's wife was an avid gardener, and he captured the chromatic brilliance of her garden in *Hollyhocks* (page 35). He spoke for many American artists when he explained his attraction to gardens, and French gardens in particular: "It is sunshine, flowers in sunshine, girls in sunshine, the nude in sunshine, which I have been principally interested in.... Not only can I paint a nude here in easy reach [in France] out of doors...but I can paint a nude in my garden or down by the fish pond and not be run out of town."

Camille Pissarro was one of the few Impressionists who chose the more humble, rustic subjects of vegetable gardens and peasants. He was influenced by earlier artists, such as Millet and Corot, who portrayed agricultural laborers. (Another French Impressionist represented in this book, Charles Angrand (*In the Garden*, page 49), also painted scenes of vegetable gardens early in his career, before he adopted the Neo-Impressionist style.) Pissarro's painting *The Vegetable Garden with Trees in Blossom, Spring, Pontoise* (page 15) is one of many he did around his home in Pontoise, a small village outside of Paris. Often called the patriarch of Impressionism, Pissarro was a dedicated teacher. Advising his son, Lucien, the elder confessed: "I recommend one thing to you, and that is always to do one's best to finish what one has begun. However, I know from my own experience the difficulty, or rather the many unexpected difficulties, that assail one while working out of doors."

America embraced Impressionism. Several exhibitions of the French Impressionists in the United States had an enormous impact. The largest and most significant of the time was the 1886 exhibition organized by the Parisian art dealer, Paul Durand-Ruel. It was held in New York City and comprised three hundred works of art: forty-eight by Monet, thirty-eight by Renoir and forty-two by Pissarro, as well as works by Mary Cassatt and Berthe Morisot. The show was a triumph. American painters energetically adopted the Impressionist aesthetic and its favorite subject, the garden.

American Impressionism contains a great diversity of expression. Its artists expanded, each in their own ways, the romantic imagery of the flower garden. For example, Childe Hassam's exuberant outdoor paintings appear closely associated with Monet's rapid, loosely painted works, and the Boston artist Robert Vonnoh clearly was influenced by Monet's canvases of fields of poppies when he painted *In Flanders Field…*(page 11). But Harry Siddons Mowbray's painting *Roses* (page 29) is imbued with elements of the sort of enigmatic symbolism favored by the Pre-Raphaelites. The female figures in this painting, garbed in exotic costumes, play dreamily upon archaic musical instruments while seated in a field of roses.

In the southern United States, Gari Melchers (1860–1932) was the leading exponent of garden painting. Born in Detroit, Melchers eventually settled in Fredericksburg, Virginia, at the beginning of World War I, after living in Weimar, West Germany, where he presided over the art academy for several years. He devoted himself to painting scenes of his own surroundings in all seasons, as evidenced in the autumnal view *In My Garden* (page 57).

Impressionism even reached as far west as California, where Joseph Raphael was its leading practitioner. Raised in California, Raphael went to Europe to live in 1903. He painted *Rhododendron Field* (page 33) in Holland or Belgium, where he spent most of his time. Raphael sent his canvases from Europe to his agent in California for exhibitions until 1939, when he and his wife returned home.

The preeminent artist working in this style in Great Britain was the American, John Singer Sargent (1856–1925). He lived most of his life in Europe, studied in Paris before settling permanently in London, visited Giverny in 1887 and became a close friend of Monet. By then Sargent had established his reputation as a London society portrait painter, but his most memorable painting is an Impressionist garden picture, *Carnation, Lily, Lily, Rose* (a detail of this painting is reproduced on page 7). Painting in the Worchestershire garden of his friend, the artist Frank Millet, Sargent worked each day for only a few minutes in the early evening, to capture those moments of special light on canvas. It took him two summers to complete the painting. Its glowing image of children in an idyllic, protected world lit by paper lanterns has a Pre-Raphaelite sensibility which appealed strongly to public taste. The painting was an immediate success and a major influence on young artists.

Many other Impressionists from both sides of the Atlantic are represented in this collection. Monet's water garden at Giverny is commemorated in the painting *Bridge at the Giverny Gardens* (page 25).

This touching homage to the master Impressionist was painted by his step-daughter, Blanche Hoschedé-Monet. She cared for Monet in his later years after the death of his second wife, and at the same time she developed as a painter and exhibited her work in Paris. Henri-Edmond Cross (French, 1856–1910) was one of a group of artists who developed a style known as Neo-Impressionism. His painting *Blossom Trees in Spring* (page 45) announces new experiments in art, with its reduced, simplified forms painted in even-sized dots of color. And although he was not an Impressionist, the eminent figure painter, Gustav Klimt, was aware of its achievements and popularity. Klimt created more than fifty landscapes, and *Roses Under the Trees* (page 47), painted in his characteristic opulent style, nevertheless reflects an Impressionist spirit.

The artists in this collection represent only a few of the many who devoted themselves to the practice of outdoor painting in the tradition that Monet, Renoir, Pissarro and their colleagues established. Some of the artists included here are relatively obscure, yet their work merits our consideration as testimony to the extent of Impressionism's penetration into our culture. It was the last art movement that reflected an untroubled world. It recorded a time of innocence, prosperity and optimism that was shattered forever with the outbreak of World War I. Today, the beauty of its warm, sweet flower gardens and poppy fields continues to lure us into its appealing, peaceful realm.

John Singer Sargent (American, 1856–1925)
Carnation, Lily, Lily, Rose (detail), 1885–6
Oil on canvas, 67½ × 59 in.
Tate Gallery, London
Photograph courtesy of The Bridgeman Art Library, London

Claude Monet (French, 1840–1926)
Gladioli, 1873
Oil on canvas, 22 × 32½ in.
© The Detroit Institute of Arts, 21.71
City of Detroit Purchase

Robert Vonnoh (American, 1858–1933)
In Flanders Field Where Soldiers Sleep and Poppies Grow, c. 1892
Oil on canvas, 58 × 104 in.
Butler Institute of American Art, Youngstown, Ohio

Philip Leslie Hale (American, 1865–1931)
The Crimson Rambler, 1908
Oil on canvas, 25¼ × 30³⁄₁₆ in.
The Pennsylvania Academy of the Fine Arts, Philadelphia
Joseph E. Temple Fund

Camille Pissarro (French, 1831–1903)
The Vegetable Garden with Trees in Blossom, Spring, Pontoise, 1877
Oil on canvas, 25⅝ × 31⅞ in.
Musée d'Orsay, Paris
Photograph courtesy of The Bridgeman Art Library, London

Childe Hassam, (American, 1859–1935)
Old House and Garden, East Hampton, Long Island, 1898
Oil on canvas, 24$\frac{1}{16}$ × 20 in.
Henry Art Gallery, University of Washington, Seattle
Horace C. Henry Collection

Pierre Auguste Renoir (French, 1841–1919)
Picking Flowers, 1875
Oil on canvas, 21⅜ × 25⅝ in.
National Gallery of Art, Washington
Ailsa Mellon Bruce Collection

Joseph Ratcliffe Skelton (British, fl. 1888-93)
A Summer Afternoon
Christopher Wood Gallery, London
Photograph courtesy of The Bridgeman Art Library, London

Claude Monet (French, 1840–1926)
The Artist's Garden at Giverny, 1900
Oil on canvas, 31⅝ × 35⅞ in.
Musée d'Orsay, Paris
Photograph courtesy of The Bridgeman Art Library, London

Blanche Hoschedé-Monet (French, 1865–1947)
Bridge at the Giverny Gardens
Rafael Valls Gallery, London
Photograph courtesy of The Bridgeman Art Library, London

Tom Mostyn (British, 1864–1930)
A Mediterranean Garden
Private Collection
Photograph courtesy of The Bridgeman Art Library, London

Henry Siddons Mowbray (American, 1858–1928)
Roses, c. 1900
Oil on canvas, 12 × 16¼ in.
National Academy of Design, New York City

Alfred de Breansky (fl. 1880–1919)
The Herbaceous Border
Christopher Wood Gallery, London
Photograph courtesy of The Bridgeman Art Library, London

Joseph Raphael (American, 1869–1950)
Rhododendron Field, 1915
Oil on canvas, 30 × 40 in.
The Oakland Museum; Gift of Dr. William S. Porter

Frederick Carl Frieseke (American, 1874–1939)
Hollyhocks, c. 1914
Oil on canvas, 25½ × 32 in.
National Academy of Design, New York City

Lucien Pissarro (French, 1863–1944)
Les Dindons
Oil on canvas
City of Bristol Museum & Art Gallery
Photograph courtesy of The Bridgeman Art Library, London

Childe Hassam (American, 1859–1935)
Geraniums, 1888–89
Oil on canvas, 18¼ × 13 in.
The Hyde Collection, Glens Falls, New York

David Woodlock

A Kentish Cottage near Edenbridge

Chris Beetles Ltd., London
Photograph courtesy of The Bridgeman Art Library, London

Edouard Gaetan Charles Ansaloni (fl. 1912–39)
The Horticulturist's Garden
Waterhouse and Dodd, London
Photograph courtesy of The Bridgeman Art Library, London

Henri-Edmond Cross (French, 1856–1910)

Blossom Trees in Spring

Oil on canvas
Ny Carlsberg Glyptotek, Copenhagen
Photograph courtesy of The Bridgeman Art Library, London

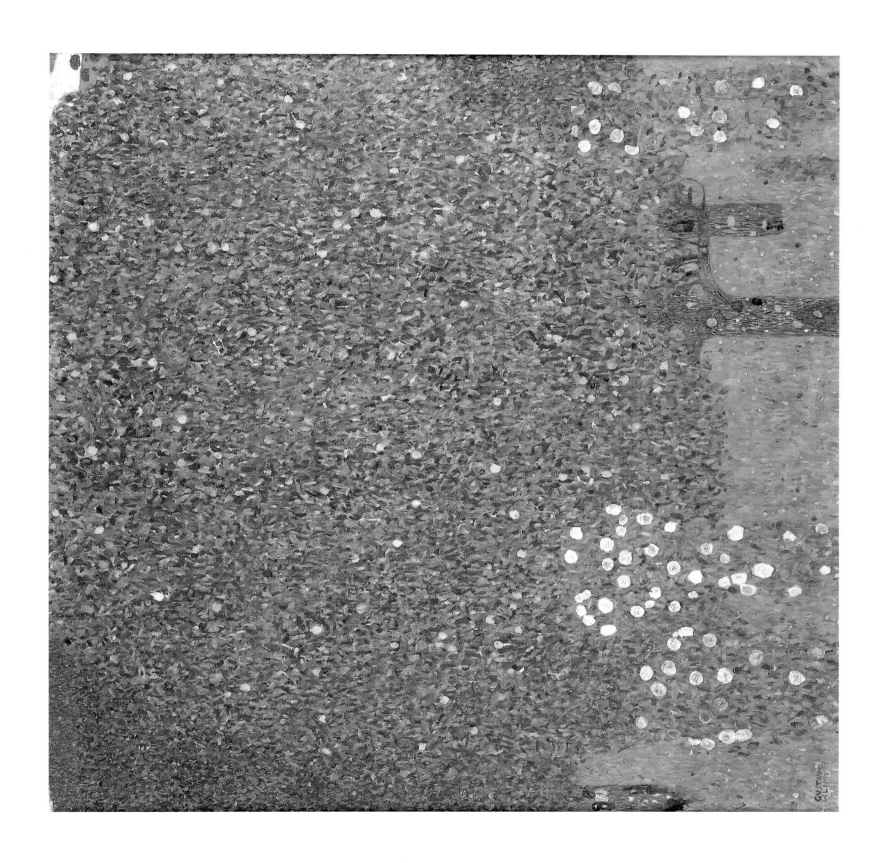

Gustav Klimt (Austrian, 1862–1918)
Roses Under the Trees, c. 1905
Oil on canvas, 43¼ × 43¼ in.
Musée d'Orsay, Paris
Photograph courtesy of The Bridgeman Art Library, London

Charles Angrand (French, 1854–1926)
In the Garden, 1885
Oil on canvas
Musée des Beaux-Arts, Rouen
Photograph courtesy of The Bridgeman Art Library, London

Johann Viktor Kramer (b. 1864)
Corfu—Cypress Trees and Oleander
Oil on canvas
Oscar & Peter Johnson Ltd., London
Photograph courtesy of The Bridgeman Art Library, London

Wynford Dewhurst (English, b. 1864)

Versailles

Oil on canvas
Gavin Graham Gallery, London
Photograph courtesy of The Bridgeman Art Library, London

Ernest Lawson (American, 1873–1939)
The Garden, 1914

Oil on canvas, 20 × 24 in.
Memorial Art Gallery of the University of Rochester
Gift of the Estate of Emily and James Sibley Watson, 1951

Gari Melchers (American, 1860–1932)
In My Garden, 1900
Oil on canvas, 41 × 40 in.
Butler Institute of American Art, Youngstown, Ohio

Childe Hassam (American, 1859–1935)
Celia Thaxter in Her Garden, 1892
Oil on canvas, 22⅛ × 18⅛ in.
National Museum of American Art, Smithsonian Institution
Gift of John Gellatly